AF335186

A Letter To My Young Melanin

Author; Carrene Bell-Stewart

Illustrations by Letsillustrate.org

All Rights reserved

Dear ,

I want you to know that you mean the world to me. You are LOVED beyond explanation. Every inch of your pure uniqueness brings NOTHING but butterflies, joy and HAPPINESS to my heart.

1

2

You are beautiful inside out. Your MELANIN is rare and so are you. Baby, the color of your skin does not define you or your future so be proud of it.

3

4

Your melanin is BOLD and
sometimes it will intimidate
others that doesn't
understand how valuable
it is to us or why we
praise and worship it.

6

Be TRUE to yourself and
what you believe in. You
can choose to be great with
NO BOUNDARIES or LIMITS. You
can be anyone you desire
to be with no restrictions.

8

Your MELANIN is beyond magical. Your soul is PURE. You were born GIFTED, blessed and appreciated. You are loved. NEVER drop your standards to please Society.

9

10

When you look out into the world I want you to see PEOPLE and not COLOR. I want you to RESPECT everyone, show COMPASSION and always LISTEN to understand and to LOVE with an open mind.

11

12

When you look in the mirror
I want you to see how
INSPIRING and breathtaking
you are. I encourage you
to be the BEST you possible. I
encourage you to make a
DIFFERENCE. I encourage you
to STAND out

14

The LIFE you have ahead of
you is an empty canvas,
paint it with SUCCESS and
make it aspiring to others
by making it your own.
Always follow your dreams.

15

There will be times where you feel doubts and that doing your best is not good enough, but NEVER give up. Hold your head up high and keep on pushing because one day it will all be worth it.

18

I love you. Thank you for showing me how to be patient and to love unconditionally. I promise to give you the best life possible, to always put you first and encourage you. I promise to set an example for you so you can grow into a brave, independent and respectable individual. I promise to protect you from all the unpleasantness this world is filled with. I promise to value you and always believed in you. I promise never to turn my back on you or to make you feel abandoned. be brave, be respectful and honest in all you do. You are my whole heart and I will forever love you.

Sign

19

CPSIA information can be obtained
at www.ICGtesting.com
Printed in the USA
LVHW072336110122
708378LV00019B/522